A SALAD A DAY

Monday's child is fair of face,
Tuesday's child is full of grace,
Wednesday's child is full of woe,
Thursday's child has far to go,
Friday's child is loving and giving,
Saturday's child works hard for a living,
And a child that is born on the Sabbath day
Is bonnie and blythe, and good and gay.

A Salad A Day

Scrumptious Salads for Every Day of the Week

Ruth Moorman & Lalla Williams

QUAIL RIDGE PRESS

Lovingly dedicated to the children,
Wickliffe and Bonnie,
Dudley and Betsy,
Randall and Pam,
Ney, Jr. and Harris

Other books by Ruth Moorman and Lalla Williams:

The Seven Chocolate Sins
The Twelve Days of Christmas Cookbook

(See page 78 for further information.)

Copyright ©1980 by
QUAIL RIDGE PRESS, INC.
Manufactured in the United States of America
First Printing, August 1980
Second Printing, May 1981
Third Printing, December 1983
ISBN 0-937552-02-X

Book design by Gwen McKee

Several illustrations inspired and adapted from drawings in the lovely children's books of English artist, Kate Greenaway, and by Eulalie in *A Child's Garden of Verses* by Robert Louis Stevenson.

CONTENTS

PREFACE

Monday's salads feature flowers—what could be "fairer of face"? The main ingredient in Tuesday's salads is poultry and its "graceful" product, the egg. The salads for Wednesday's "woes" try to brighten the day with colorful vegetables. Thursday's meat salads supply protein for the one who "has far to go." The traditional food for Friday is fish, so the salads are seafood. It is also Freyja's Day, the Scandinavian goddess of love, so the salads are generous enough to be "lovingly shared." Saturday's meals-in-a-dish—a salad bowl this time—make light work of cooking and dishwashing. So for the one who "works hard for a living," these salads are complete meals. For Sunday, the "bonnie" fruit salads are so "good," you may choose to serve them for dessert!

Most salads have lettuce or leafy greens. These should be soaked in salted water about ten minutes, rinsed thoroughly and drained. Tear, never cut up the greens, put them in a bowl, cover with a paper towel and refrigerate.

Since salad making is a creative art, there are no rules to limit your adding an extra ingredient or substituting another dressing for any of the recipes.

For your enjoyment, your shape, your health—have yourself *A Salad A Day!*

Ruth Moorman and Lalla Williams

Monday's Child

is fair of face

Who feels "fair of face" on a blue Monday morning? But if Monday noon brings you face to face with one of these lovely flower salads, Monday will turn "sky blue." Go sparingly with the pepper on these salads, for "if you sneeze on Monday, you sneeze for danger." Be sure to use only flowers that have had no systemic fertilizer in beds near them. For this reason, it is best to use only the flowers from your own fair garden.

Flowers

Lilies of the Field
Maytime Monday
Hawaiian Garden
Tulip Cups
Bright Circle
Bits of Sunshine
Golden Flowers
Portia's Pride
Pretty as a Rose
Lion's Tooth
Honey Glow Salad

7

LILIES OF THE FIELD

1 cup fresh peaches, sliced
½ cup day lily blossoms,
  (hermerocallis)

Bibb lettuce, torn small
Yogurt Dressing

Lightly toss the peaches, lily blossoms and lettuce with the dressing.

MAYTIME MONDAY

1 cup nasturtium leaves and
  flowers
1 head lettuce, shredded

½ cup watercress
1 tablespoon mint
French Dressing

Add *French Dressing* to all other ingredients. A delicately different salad.

HAWAIIAN GARDEN

Fresh pineapple, split lengthwise
Fresh fruit
Champagne or orange liqueur

Poppy Seed dressing
Gardenia blossoms

Scoop out pineapple and chop the fruit. Add the pineapple to other fresh fruit of your choice and marinate the fruits in champagne or the orange liqueur until chilled. Drain. Fill the pineapple halves with the fruit and pour on a little *Poppy Seed* dressing. Surround with gardenias on a pretty plate. Tropically delicious!

TULIP CUPS

PINK TULIPS (with stamen and pistils removed):

1 cup strawberries, halved   *1 tablespoon honey*
1 cup honeydew melon balls   *½ cup whipped topping*
¼ cup sour cream   *Lettuce*

Combine the strawberries and melon balls in a dressing made by blending the remaining ingredients. Carefully fill the tulip blossoms and arrange on lettuce.

YELLOW TULIPS (with stamen and pistils removed):

1 cup fresh pineapple, chopped   *1 cup orange or manderin sections*

Combine the pineapple and orange sections in the above dressing and carefully fill the tulip blossoms. Serve on lettuce. A colorful springtime sensation.

Monday/Flowers

9

BRIGHT CIRCLE

Cucumber, thinly sliced
Nasturtium blossoms and small
  leaves, washed and blotted dry

French Dressing *with a pinch of*
  mixed herbs

Marinate cucumber in dressing at least an hour. Place in a dish and surround with flowers and leaves.

BITS OF SUNSHINE

1 tablespoon plain gelatin
3 tablespoons cold water
¼ cup boiling water
¼ cup blue cheese
½ cup sour cream
½ cup cream

1 tablespoon sherry
¼ cup bell pepper, finely chopped
¼ cup marigold petals
Lettuce
Marigold blossoms

Soften gelatin in cold water and then dissolve it in boiling water. Blend together the cheese, creams, and sherry. Add gelatin to mixture. Cool. Lightly stir in bell pepper and flowers. Pour into a mold and chill until set. Unmold on lettuce and garnish with remaining flowers.

GOLDEN FLOWERS

1 cup chrysanthemum petals
Bibb lettuce
1 orange, thinly sliced

1 cup fresh pineapple, chopped
Celery Seed or Poppy Seed
Dressing

Toss the chrysanthemum petals, torn lettuce, peeled orange slices, and pineapple with one of the dressings.

PORTIA'S PRIDE

Cherry tomatoes, skinned and
  halved
Bibb lettuce
French Dressing

Fresh young leaves of portulaca
  oleracea (purslane), stems re-
  moved

Arrange tomatoes on bed of lettuce. Garnish with leaves and pour on dressing.

PRETTY AS A ROSE

Strawberry Sunrise or Poppy Seed
  Dressing
2 cups Kiwi fruit, sliced

1 banana, sliced
Rose petals

Lightly combine dressing with fruit. Place on four salad plates and surround with rose petals. Pretty and delicious.

LION'S TOOTH

Dandelion leaves
1 apple, thinly sliced
1 tablespoon finely chopped onion

¼ cup pecans or walnuts
French Dressing

Combine dandelion leaves, apple slices, onion and pecans. Mix lightly with *French Dressing*.

HONEY GLOW SALAD

1 tablespoon honey
¼ cup orange juice
1 teaspoon lemon juice
1 carrot, grated
1 apple, diced

1 tablespoon raisins
1 tablespoon celery, chopped
¼ cup sunflower seeds
1 cup cottage cheese

Blend the honey and juices. Combine with remaining ingredients. Deliciously nutritious!

Tuesday's Child
is full of grace

A chicken may not be graceful, but who can deny that the egg it lays has a graceful shape? Since poultry and eggs are included in almost every dieter's grocery list, when you try these salads, *your* shape may grow more graceful. Some of them can be used for sandwich fillings—on thin-sliced bread, of course!

Poultry & Eggs

Confetti Egg Salad
Eggs en Gelée
Tuesday Mousse
Hens and Chickens
Peachy Good
Grapeful Chicken
Curried Chicken Salad
Chicken Pecan Salad
Cranberry Ring
Gaudy Dutch
Cool Chicken Clemenceau
China Trade
Frances' Christmas Salad
Tangy Turkey Salad
Macaroni Mardi

CONFETTI EGG SALAD

6 hardcooked eggs, chopped
½ cup finely chopped celery
½ cup chopped green olives
½ cup pimentos, chopped
Salt and pepper

Few drops hot sauce
Dash of curry powder
½ cup mayonnaise or more
Spinach leaves
Whole stuffed olives

Combine first 8 ingredients and fold together. Serve on beds of spinach topped with whole stuffed olives.

EGGS EN GELEE

1½ cups bouillon
1 tablespoon plain gelatin
Juice of ½ lemon
3 hardcooked eggs

Durkee's salad dressing
Mustard
Salt and pepper

Soften the gelatin in one-half cup of bouillon and cook over low heat until dissolved. Add the remaining bouillon and lemon juice. Pour aspic to the level of one-half inch in a Pyrex dish and chill. Halve the eggs lengthwise and mash the yolks, seasoning them with the Durkee's and mustard; salt and pepper to taste. Stuff into the whites. When the aspic has begun to thicken, arrange the eggs on it and cover with the remainder of the aspic. Chill until firm. Cut in squares around eggs. A garnish of parsley may be used around the eggs. Serves 6.

TUESDAY MOUSSE

2 tablespoons butter	½ cup heavy cream, whipped
2 tablespoons flour	6 hardcooked eggs, chopped
1 cup milk	¼ cup celery, finely chopped
Onion salt and white pepper	½ cup diced cucumber
1 tablespoon plain gelatin	¼ cup mayonnaise
¼ cup white wine	½ teaspoon Worcestershire sauce
¼ cup boiling water	Salt

Melt butter and gently cook flour in butter for 2 minutes. Add milk and cook, stirring, until mixture thickens. Season. Soften gelatin in wine and dissolve it in boiling water. Blend gelatin into cream sauce. Fold in whipped cream. Lightly combine eggs, celery, cucumber with mayonnaise. Season. Fold egg mixture into gelatin cream. Pour into a mold and chill until set.

HENS AND CHICKENS

6 hardcooked eggs	1 cup hot chicken stock
1 boiled hen, meat removed and cut to bite size	1 cup boiled shrimp
1 tablespoon plain gelatin	Garnish: Lettuce, tomatoes, mayonnaise, ripe olives

Separate the egg yolks and whites and finely chop each. Lightly oil a loaf pan and layer the bottom with the chicken, then yolks, then whites. Arrange the shrimp on the top. Dissolve the gelatin in the cold water and stir into hot chicken stock. Allow to cool slightly and pour over the loaf. Refrigerate until set. Serve on lettuce garnished with tomato wedges, a spoonful of mayonnaise and a pitted ripe olive.

PEACHY GOOD

2 cups cooked chicken, diced
1 cup peaches, sliced
½ cup bell pepper, thinly sliced
½ cup sour cream

½ cup salad dressing
Salt and white pepper
Lettuce

Combine the first three ingredients in a dressing made by blending the sour cream with the salad dressing. Season and chill. Serve on a bed of lettuce.

GRAPEFUL CHICKEN

2 cups cooked chicken, cut in
  bite-size pieces
1 cup finely chopped celery
¾ cup slivered almonds

1 cup mayonnaise
½ cup sour cream
¼ cup whipping cream, whipped
2 cups seedless grapes

Put the first three ingredients into a large bowl. Combine the mayonnaise, sour cream and whipping cream in a small bowl. Pour over the chicken mixture and fold together lightly. Add 1 cup of grapes which have been halved. Serve on beds of salad greens and garnish with remaining grapes. Serves 6.

CURRIED CHICKEN SALAD

3 cups cooked chicken, cut
  in bite-size pieces
1 cup finely chopped tart apple,
  peeled
1 cup celery, finely chopped

1 cup heavy cream
1 cup homemade mayonnaise
1 teaspoon curry powder
Salt and pepper to taste
Lettuce and fresh orange sections

Combine the first 3 ingredients. Mix the remaining ingredients together, add to the first and fold together. Serve on beds of lettuce. Freshly prepared orange sections may be added to each serving as a garnish. Serves 6.

CHICKEN PECAN SALAD

2 cups sliced fresh peaches
3 cups cooked chicken, cut in
  bite-size pieces
1 cup chopped celery
½ cup mayonnaise (homemade,
  if possible)

2 tablespoons salad oil
1 tablespoon lemon juice
½ teaspoon salt
½ cup broken pecans which
  have been toasted
Parsley

Reserve a few peach slices for garnish. Combine remaining peaches, chicken and celery. In a small bowl, mix mayonnaise, oil, lemon juice and salt. Pour over the chicken mixture and fold together lightly. Fold in the pecans. Serve in the center of a cranberry ring and garnish with a few peach slices and chopped parsley.

CRANBERRY RING

2 cups fresh orange juice
1 cup water
2 (3-ounce) packages lemon
  gelatin

¼ teaspoon salt
1 (1-pound) can whole cranberry
  sauce

Heat 1 cup of orange juice and 1 cup of water to the boiling point. Add the gelatin and salt and stir until the gelatin is dissolved. Stir in one additional cup of orange juice and chill until partially set. Stir in cranberry sauce. Pour into a 6-cup ring mold. Chill several hours. Unmold on a large serving plate.

GAUDY DUTCH

6 hardcooked eggs, cut up
2 cans pickled beets, drained
  and cut up
3 green onions, finely chopped

Mayonnaise
¼ cup chopped dill
Salt and pepper
Spinach greens

Combine first six ingredients and chill. Serve on beds of fresh spinach greens. Gaudy and good!

COOL CHICKEN CLEMENCEAU

1 cup cooked chicken, diced
1½ cups cooked brown and wild
  rice
½ cup sliced mushrooms

½ cup fresh or frozen English
  peas, cooked
Vinaigrette dressing
Lemon pepper

Combine the first five ingredients and season. Substitute white wine for lemon juice in *Vinaigrette* dressing recipe. Add dressing to chicken and toss to mix. Chill before serving.

CHINA TRADE

2 cups cooked chicken, chopped
2 apples, chopped
1 carrot, grated
2 hardcooked eggs, chopped
¼ cup raisins

4 teaspoons finely chopped onion
Mayonnaise
Curry powder
Salt and white pepper

Combine mayonnaise with curry powder to taste. Lightly stir in the first 6 ingredients and season. Serve on lettuce. Good with crackers or toast points.

FRANCES' CHRISTMAS SALAD

FIRST LAYER:

1 tablespoon gelatin
¼ cup cold water
¼ cup boiling water
½ cup mayonnaise
½ cup cream

1½ cups cooked turkey, chopped
1 (8½-ounce) can water chestnuts,
   thinly sliced
½ cup celery, chopped
¼ cup bell pepper, chopped

Soften gelatin in cold water and dissolve in boiling water. Blend gelatin into mayonnaise and cream. Fold in turkey and vegetables. Pour into a mold and chill until almost firm.

SECOND LAYER:

1 tablespoon gelatin
¼ cup cold water
½ cup sugar
Dashes of cloves and cinnamon
¾ cup water

1 (1-pound) can whole cranberries
1 tablespoon orange rind, grated
Sour cream
Parsley

Soften gelatin in cold water. Combine sugar and spices in a saucepan. Stir in water and heat, stirring until almost boiling. Remove from heat. Add gelatin and stir until dissolved. Add cranberries and orange rind. Cool and then pour onto first layer. Chill thoroughly. Serve garnished with sour cream and parsley.

TANGY TURKEY SALAD

2 cups cooked turkey, diced
½ cup celery, chopped
½ cup mayonnaise
3 tablespoons chili sauce

1 teaspoon lemon juice
½ teaspoon horseradish
¼ teaspoon Worcestershire
2 drops Tabasco

Combine the turkey and celery in a dressing made by blending the sour cream with the salad dressing. Season and chill. Serve on a bed of lettuce.

MACARONI MARDI

12 ounces cooked maraconi,
    drained
12 hardcooked eggs, chopped
1 tiny onion, chopped finely

1 large can tiny peas, undrained
1 cup Miracle Whip
Salt and pepper

Lightly mix all ingredients together in a large bowl. Great take-along to barbeques and picnics.

Wednesday's Child is full of woe

These colorful vegetable salads will chase away woe even for Wednesday's child. Since according to Bishop Ussher the world was created on a Wednesday, and soon after people started eating apples, you will find some apple in *Eve's Slaw*.

Vegetables

Artichokes Plus
Bright and Beautiful
Caesar Salad
Green Beans and Artichokes
Luxury Salad
Woe-Be-Gone Salad
Asparagus Glacé
Wilted Wednesday
Beautiful Parsley
Spring Garden
Ruby Wednesday
Bonnie Beet Salad
Tomatoes au Gratin
Never On Sunday
Comes The Sun
Dressy Broccoli
Nirvana

Three Bean Salad
Boston Bean Salad
Overnite Salad
Winter Solstice
New Year's Salad for John Minary
Goldenrod
Eve's Slaw
Parmesan Cabbage
Kaiser Salad
Red Hot Cabbage Salad
Fresh Beginning
Red and Green
Basic Tomato Aspic
Kentucky Tomatoes
Summer Cooler
Tipsy Avocados
Avocado Souffle

Robin's Song
Sunlit Carrots
Perfect Day Potato Salad
Heather's Cheddar Cheese Salad

ARTICHOKES PLUS

4 artichokes	1 (4-ounce) can mushrooms
2 green onions, finely chopped	1 (3¾-ounce) can smoked oysters
1 clove garlic, minced	1 teaspoon parsley, finely
2 tablespoons oil	chopped
2 tablespoons white wine	1 teaspoon Worcestershire sauce
1 teaspoon lemon juice	Few dashes Tabasco
3 slices fresh whole wheat bread,	Salt and lemon pepper
cubed	

Boil artichokes in salted water until a leaf can be easily pulled out, about 40 minutes. Meanwhile, make dressing by sauteing onions and garlic in oil till tender. Pour wine and lemon juice over bread to soften. Stir bread and liquids into onions and combine thoroughly over low heat until there is a thick consistency. Add mushrooms, oysters and parsley. Season with sauce, Tabasco, and lemon pepper. Drain artichokes and remove center leaves to get to the base. Scrape out fibrous center. Fill with dressing.

BRIGHT AND BEAUTIFUL

1 bunch fresh broccoli	¾ cup mayonnaise
2 carrots, shaved with a potato	½ cup heavy cream
peeler	1 tablespoon sugar
1 cup celery, finely chopped	1 teaspoon salt
6 green onions, finely chopped	Fresh cracked pepper

Soak broccoli in cold salted water for 10 minutes. Drain and cut off tough portion of stalk. Cut up remaining broccoli. Place in a bowl with carrots, celery and onions. Combine mayonnaise, heavy cream, sugar, salt and pepper. Pour over vegetables and toss lightly.

CAESAR SALAD

1 head iceberg lettuce
1 head Boston lettuce
½ cup grated Parmesan cheese
2 teaspoons capers
Butter Churn Croutons
¾ cup olive oil

2 tablespoons tarragon vinegar
1 tablespoon lemon juice
1 teaspoon mustard
Fresh ground black pepper
2 eggs, coddled one minute
1 clove garlic, split

Rub a large wooden salad bowl with a split clove of garlic. Place washed and chilled greens in the bowl, adding the cheese, capers and croutons. Mix the oil, vinegar, lemon juice, mustard and pepper together. Just before serving, break the eggs into the dressing and stir well. Pour over the salad and toss. Serves six.

GREEN BEANS AND ARTICHOKES

3 cans whole green beans
1 can artichoke hearts, cut in
  halves
1 red onion, thinly sliced

1 teaspoon salt
1½ cups sugar
1 cup vinegar
1½ cups salad oil

Drain beans and artichokes. Combine other ingredients, stirring until sugar is dissolved in vinegar and oil. Add beans and artichokes. Let stand 24 hours. Especially good with a bowl of hot bean soup!

LUXURY SALAD

1 cup Gruyere cheese, cubed
½ cup mushrooms
½ cup pecans

½ cup watercress
Vinaigrette dressing
Lettuce, shredded

Combine the first 5 ingredients and serve on a bed of lettuce.

WOE-BE-GONE SALAD

1 cup new potatoes, cooked and
  sliced
1 cup French-style green beans,
  cooked and drained
½ cup red Delicious apple, diced
¼ cup celery, chopped

½ cup mayonnaise
2 tablespoons sour cream
1 tablespoon lemon juice
½ teaspoon horseradish
Salt and pepper

Combine the ingredients in the first column with a dressing made by mixing the ingredients in the second column.

ASPARAGUS GLACE

1 tablespoon plain gelatin
¼ cup cold water
1¾ cups beef bouillon

3 eggs, hardcooked and sliced
1 (8¼-ounce) can asparagus tips
Lettuce and mayonnaise

Soften gelatin in cold water. Bring bouillon to a boil and stir in gelatin until dissolved. Chill until gelatin begins to thicken. Pour a thin layer of bouillon into a mold and arrange the egg slices in the bouillon. Chill until bouillon begins to set. Carefully fold in asparagus tips into the remaining thickened bouillon and pour onto egg layer. Chill until set. Serve on lettuce and garnish with mayonnaise.

WILTED WEDNESDAY

4 slices bacon
¼ cup vinegar
1½ teaspoons sugar
Salt and pepper

2 tablespoons green onion,
  chopped
Bibb lettuce, spinach or other
  leafy greens, roughly torn

Fry bacon until crisp. Remove bacon and drain it, reserving 2 tablespoons bacon drippings. Stir vinegar, sugar, and seasoning into pan and bring to a boil. Stir in chopped onion and gradually add lettuce. Stir lettuce until it is slightly wilted. Crumble bacon and add. Serve immediately.

BEAUTIFUL PARSLEY

2 cups Number 2 wheat
5 large tomatoes cut up into
  very small pieces
1 bunch finely chopped green
  onions
2 bunches of parsley, washed,
  dried and finely cut with scissors

½ cup finely cut mint leaves
1 cup olive oil
4 tablespoons lemon juice
Salt
Coarsely ground pepper
Lettuce or spinach leaves

Wash wheat in cold water. Drain. Cover with more cold water and soak until the water has been absorbed. Combine with the remaining ingredients. Serve on lettuce or spinach leaves. Serves ten.

SPRING GARDEN

Basic Tomato Aspic *Ring*
Radishes, thinly sliced
Fresh asparagus, cooked
Spring peas, cooked
Zuchini or crookneck squash,
  thinly sliced
Green onion, chopped

CREAM DRESSING:
8 ounces cream cheese
1 tablespoon cream
2 tablespoons orange juice
½ teaspoon prepared mustard
1 teaspoon mint, minced

Surround the aspic ring with the vegetables and fill the center with the *Cream Dressing*.

Wednesday/Vegetables

RUBY WEDNESDAY

1 cup beets, cooked and thinly
  sliced
½ cup carrots, cooked and diced
½ cup peas, cooked

½ cup potatoes, cooked and diced
¼ cup French Dressing
Salt and pepper
¼ cup mayonnaise

Toss vegetables with *French Dressing*. Season and chill thoroughly.
Gently stir in mayonnaise.

BONNIE BEET SALAD

1 cup beets, cooked and thinly
  sliced
¼ cup Vinaigrette *dressing*

½ teaspoon caraway seeds
Lettuce
Sour cream

Marinate the beets in the dressing with the caraway seeds.
Chill thoroughly. Serve on lettuce and garnish with sour
cream.

TOMATOES AU GRATIN

4 thick slices of large summer
  tomato
4 slices processed Swiss cheese

4 slices Bermuda onion
Lettuce
French Dressing

Arrange the first 4 ingredients in order on a bed of lettuce.
Cover with dressing.

NEVER ON SUNDAY

1 large tomato, skinned, chopped
2 green onions, chopped
¼ cup feta cheese, crumbled

8 black olives, sliced
Vinaigrette *dressing*
Anchovies

Lightly combine the tomato, onion, cheese, and olives with
the dressing. Garnish with anchovies.

COMES THE SUN

1 (1-pound) can whole green
  beans, drained
Vinaigrette dressing
4 strips bacon

2 eggs, hardcooked
2 tablespoons mayonnaise
1 teaspoon lemon juice

Marinate the beans in *Vinaigrette* and chill. Fry bacon until crisp and crumble it. Chop the egg whites and mix with mayonnaise and lemon juice. Arrange beans like spokes around a center of egg white mixture. Sprinkle the bacon onto the beans, and sieve the egg yolks over all. Scrumptious and sunny!

DRESSY BROCCOLI

Lettuce
1 cup chopped broccoli, cooked
2 eggs, hardcooked and cut into
  wedges
1 green onion, finely chopped
Anchovies

½ cup French Dressing
1 tablespoon dill pickle, finely
  chopped
1 tablespoon parsley, finely
  cut with scissors

On a bed of lettuce, arrange broccoli and egg wedges. Garnish with green onion and anchovies. Cover with *French Dressing*. Sprinkle dill pickle and parsley over all.

NIRVANA

3 eggs, hardcooked and chopped
2 green onions, finely chopped
1 small jar pimento, chopped
1 cup very sharp cheese, shaved

½ cup sliced water chestnuts
2 large cans English peas, drained
1 tablespoon toasted poppy seed
Mayonnaise and lettuce

Fold first 6 ingredients together with as much mayonnaise as desired. Refrigerate overnight to allow seasoning to penetrate. Serve on lettuce beds. Garnish with poppy seeds.

THREE BEAN SALAD

1 small onion, finely chopped
1 small bell pepper, finely chopped
¾ cup sugar
1 teaspoon salt
½ teaspoon black pepper

¼ cup salad oil
¾ cup apple cider vinegar
1 can wax beans
1 can green beans
1 can red kidney beans

Combine first 7 ingredients and mix well. Drain the beans and add to the first mixture. Toss thoroughly and allow to stand overnight before serving.

BOSTON BEAN SALAD

1 cup canned baked beans
¼ cup celery, chopped
1 tablespoon bell pepper, chopped
1 teaspoon onion, finely chopped

½ teaspoon prepared mustard
1 tablespoon Vinaigrette dressing
3 strips bacon

Combine the first 6 ingredients and chill. Fry bacon until crisp and drain. Crumble bacon over beans before serving.

OVERNITE SALAD

1 head iceberg lettuce
¼ head red cabbage
Salt and pepper
2 tablespoons sugar
1 package frozen English peas
8 slices bacon, fried crisp

6 green onions, finely chopped
2 cups sharp cheese, grated
1½ cups mayonnaise
½ cup sour cream
Parsley

Wash the lettuce and cabbage and allow to drain. Tear the lettuce, shred the cabbage and put into a large serving bowl. Sprinkle with salt, pepper and sugar. Add peas, crumbled bacon, onion and cheese in one layer for each ingredient. Combine the mayonnaise and sour cream and spread on top, covering the entire salad to the edge of the bowl. Garnish with parsley and allow to stand in refrigerator a full 24 hours before serving.

WINTER SOLSTICE

½ head iceberg lettuce, shredded
Mustard greens
Spinach greens
Parsley flakes

Green onion, finely chopped,
   including tops
Oil and Vinegar dressing
2 hardcooked eggs, finely diced

Wash and drain all greens and allow to chill in the refrigerator. When they are crisp, combine with the parsley flakes,
Oil and Vinegar dressing and toss. Serve on plates or in salad
bowls and garnish with hardcooked eggs.

NEW YEAR'S SALAD FOR JOHN MINARY

2 teaspoons onion, minced
2 teaspoons wine vinegar
2 tablespoons salad oil
4 tablespoons cream

1 cup cooked black-eyed peas
Salt and pepper
3 strips bacon
Parsley

Blend the first four ingredients. Add the peas and season. Chill
thoroughly. Fry bacon until crisp and drain. Before serving,
crumble bacon over the beans and garnish with parsley.

GOLDENROD

2 cups canned kidney beans,
   drained
¼ cup onion, thinly sliced
2 tablespoons dill pickle, finely
   chopped
2 eggs, hardcooked

½ cup celery, sliced
¼ cup Cheddar cheese, grated
½ cup mayonnaise
1 tablespoon liquid from dill
   pickles
Salt and pepper

Combine beans, celery, onion, pickle and chopped egg white
with mayonnaise. Add dill pickle juice. Season and garnish
with sieved egg yolk.

EVE'S SLAW

1 cup cabbage, shredded
¼ cup carrot, grated
¼ cup celery, chopped
½ cup apple, diced
¼ cup bell pepper, finely chopped
¼ cup peanuts, chopped

½ cup sour cream
1 tablespoon lemon juice
1 tablespoon wine vinegar
1 tablespoon sugar
¼ teaspoon dry mustard
Salt and black pepper

Combine the ingredients in the first column in the dressing made by blending the next 5 ingredients. Season and chill.

PARMESAN CABBAGE

½ cup mayonnaise
¼ cup whole milk
2 tablespoons grated Parmesan
   cheese
1 tablespoon white vinegar
1 teaspoon lemon juice

½ teaspoon dillweed
Few dashes garlic powder
¼ teaspoon salt
1 head Savoy cabbage
Parsley

In a small bowl combine all ingredients, reserving the cabbage. Blend together with a wire whisk. Slice through the cabbage making individual servings. Place on salad plates and pour on the dressing. Garnish with parsley.

KAISER SALAD

1 (16-ounce) can sauerkraut
¼ cup onion, finely chopped
¼ cup bell pepper
¼ cup celery, chopped
2 tablespoons pimento, chopped

¼ cup salad oil
¼ cup vinegar
¼ cup sugar
Salt and pepper

Combine the vegetables in a mixture of oil, vinegar and sugar. Season and chill thoroughly.

RED HOT CABBAGE SALAD

3 tablespoons salad oil
6 cups (1 large head) shredded
  red cabbage
3 cups unpared apple, cut up
¼ cup brown sugar, firmly packed

¼ cup water
¼ cup vinegar
1½ teaspoons salt
Pepper to taste

Heat the oil in a skillet. Add the remaining ingredients and cook over moderate heat, uncovered, stirring constantly. Cook for approximately 15 minutes or less depending upon the crispness desired. Serves six.

FRESH BEGINNING

6 tablespoons salad oil
2 tablespoons vinegar
1 teaspoon sugar
½ teaspoon mustard
1 cup sprouted grain or beans

2 green onions, finely chopped
2 tablespoons pimento, chopped
1 tablespoon parsley, finely
  chopped
Salt and pepper

Blend the oil, vinegar, sugar, and mustard to make the dressing. Combine the sprouts, onions, pimento and parsley with the dressing and season. Chill before serving.

RED AND GREEN

2 cups zucchini, cooked, sliced   1 tablespoon chives or parsley
2 tomatoes, skinned, thinly sliced   Vinaigrette dressing

Arrange the zucchini and tomato slices on a dish. Pour on dressing and garnish with chives or parsley.

BASIC TOMATO ASPIC

1 tablespoon gelatin   ¼ teaspoon Worcestershire sauce
3 tablespoons cold water   ¼ teaspoon sugar
2 cups tomato juice   Salt
1 teaspoon lemon juice

Soften the gelatin in cold water. Bring the tomato juice to a boil. Dissolve the gelatin in the juice. Add lemon juice, Worcestershire sauce, sugar, and season with salt. Pour into a mold and chill until set.

KENTUCKY TOMATOES

6 tomatoes   2 tablespoons celery, chopped
1 (½-pint) carton cottage cheese   Salt and pepper
1 teaspoon parsley, minced   French Dressing
2 tablespoons bell pepper, chopped

Remove the tops of the tomatoes and cut into quarters half way down. Combine the cottage cheese with the vegetables and season to taste. Fill tomatoes with cheese mixture and pour on *French Dressing*. Serves 6.

SUMMER COOLER

2 cups cucumbers, diced   1 tablespoon mint, chopped
½ cup yogurt   Lettuce
½ cup pecans, chopped

Combine the first 4 ingredients and serve on a bed of lettuce.

TIPSY AVOCADOS

Avocados   Salt and pepper
Dry Madeira   Pecans, chopped

Split avocados and remove seed. With a fork, scratch into the
avocado and pour in a little wine. Season and garnish with
pecans. Serve immediately.

AVOCADO SOUFFLE

1 tablespoon plain gelatin   ¼ teaspoon salt
3 tablespoons cold water   2 cups avocados, peeled and cut
½ cup boiling water   into chunks
1 tablespoon lemon juice   Lettuce
2 eggs, separated   Garnish: black olives, lemon slices
1 (3-ounce) package cream cheese,   grapefruit sections or sliced
   cut into small pieces, softened   tomatoes

Soften gelatin in cold water and dissolve in boiling water.
Add lemon juice. Beat egg whites till stiff; beat egg yolks
till light. Beat cream cheese and avocados into egg yolks until
smooth. Add dissolved gelatin and salt. Fold egg whites into
avocados and pour into a mold. Chill till set. Serve on lettuce
and garnish with a thin slice of lemon and a couple of black
olives, or with grapefruit sections, or a slice of tomato.

ROBIN'S SONG

Lettuce   Hardcooked eggs, chopped
Hearts of palm   Mandarin orange sections
Beets   Dressing

Arrange hearts of palm, beets and mandarin orange sections
on beds of crisp lettuce. Sprinkle eggs over lightly. Good with
Secret Spring, Green Goddess, Avocado II, or *French*.

SUNLIT CARROTS

2 pounds carrots
1 cup tomato soup, undiluted
¼ cup salad oil
½ cup honey
¾ cup vinegar

1 green pepper, quarter-ring sliced
1 large onion, quarter-ring sliced
1 teaspoon mustard
1 teaspoon Worcestershire

Cook peeled, sliced carrots until not quite tender. Drain and cool, then marinate in remaining ingredients in refrigerator overnight. Keeps well if they last!

PERFECT DAY POTATO SALAD

8 medium potatoes
3 eggs
5 stalks celery, finely chopped
4 tablespoons sweet relish

1 teaspoon grated onion
Salt, pepper, paprika to taste
¾ cup mayonnaise
½ cup sour cream

Boil potatoes with eggs about 25 minutes or till fork pierces easily—do not overcook. Drain and refrigerate. When cold, peel potatoes and cut into uniform small cubes. Shell and finely chop eggs. In a large bowl, mix all ingredients except mayonnaise and sour cream with a fork. Lastly coat lightly with mayonnaise and sour cream. For a different flavor, try *Salad Cream* as an alternate dressing.

HEATHER'S CHEDDAR CHEESE SALAD

½ head lettuce
½ cup grated Cheddar cheese
1 large tomato, cut into small
  pieces

Handful Butter Churn Croutons
2 tablespoons bacon bits
Salt and pepper
Italian Dressing

Toss torn lettuce that has been washed and crisped with remaining ingredients. Ten-year old Heather concocted this and it has become a family favorite!

Thursday's Child has far to go

Thursday is Thor's Day; in French it is *Jeudi*, Jove's Day. Both Thor and Jove are gods of thunder. If one has far to go on a dark and stormy Thursday, a delicious *Daube Glace* or *London Pub* salad will help get one there. Do not wait until three Thursdays come together (never!) to treat yourself to the *Three Thursdays Salad*.

Meats

Hot Roast Beef Salad
Simple Daube Glacé
Neapolitan Salad
London Pub
Janet's Taco Fiesta
Ham Pastiche
Porky-Pine Salad
Bacon and Egg Salad
Rhineland Rainbow
Three Thursdays Salad
Lightning Quick Salad
Greens au Gratin
Hawaiian Ham Salad
Far-To-Go Salad

HOT ROAST BEEF SALAD

2 cups cooked roast beef cubes	1 cup mayonnaise
1¼ cups coarsely chopped celery	1 teaspoon Worcestershire
½ cup coarsely chopped bell	½ teaspoon soy sauce
pepper	½ cup shaved American cheese
½ cup sliced water chestnuts	¾ cup Ritz Cracker crumbs
½ teaspoon grated onion	

Combine the ingredients, reserving the cheese and crumbs, and mix together. Place in a greased casserole and cover with the cheese and crumbs. Heat just until bubbly. Serves six.

SIMPLE DAUBE GLACE

1½ cups beef bouillon	8 - 10 thin slices roast beef
1 tablespoon plain gelatin	Lettuce
1 teaspoon sherry, brandy, OR	Horseradish Sauce
lemon juice	

Sprinkle the gelatin over one half cup of bouillon. Cook and stir over low heat until the gelatin has dissolved. Add remaining bouillon and preferred seasoning. Pour mixture into a chilled mold to the depth of about one half inch. Allow this to chill until lightly firm. Arrange thinly-sliced pieces of well done roast beef in overlapping pattern. Pour the remainder of the aspic over the meat and chill. Serve on lettuce beds and dress with *Horseradish Sauce*.

NEAPOLITAN SALAD

Lettuce	½ cup salami, Julienne sliced
Watercress	1 carrot, grated
2 tomatoes, sliced	Vinaigrette dressing
½ cup cucumber, thinly sliced	

Make a bed of lettuce and watercress. Arrange tomatoes, cucumbers, and salami on greens. Sprinkle grated carrot over and pour on dressing.

LONDON PUB

12 slices cooked roast veal
2 eggs, hardcooked and sliced
1 tablespoon plain gelatin
3 tablespoons cold water
1½ cups chicken broth
1 tablespoon white wine

1 tablespoon parsley, finely
  chopped
1 teaspoon onion, finely chopped
1 teaspoon horseradish-mustard
Lettuce
Mayonnaise or Salad Cream

Soften gelatin in cold water. Heat broth to the boil and dissolve gelatin in it. Cool. Add wine. Blend the ham, parsley, onion, and horseradish-mustard and spread on the veal slices. Arrange veal slices in a mold and put egg slices on top. Pour in gelatin and chill until set. Garnish with mayonnaise or *Salad Cream.*

JANET'S TACO FIESTA

1 pound ground meat
¼ teaspoon onion
1 package Taco seasoning mix
1 can red kidney beans, drained
½ large head lettuce, torn

1 tomato, cut in pieces
¼ pound grated sharp cheese
½ large bag crushed Dorito chips
1 cup Thousand Island *dressing*

Brown meat with onion powder. Add Taco mix and beans. Stir. Remove from burner and set aside. Mix chopped tomato, cheese and Dorito chips in large salad bowl. Add ground meat mixture, then *Thousand Island* dressing. Toss lettuce in last and serve immediately. A Mexican meal in a bowl!

HAM PASTICHE

1 cup cooked pasta shells
½ cup ham, chopped
½ cup Cheddar cheese, cubed
½ cup black olives, sliced

¼ cup bell pepper, finely chopped
1 teaspoon prepared mustard
½ cup mayonnaise
Salt and pepper

Combine first five ingredients in a dressing made by blending the mustard into mayonnaise. Season and chill.

PORKY-PINE SALAD

2 cups leftover pork, cut up   ½ cup chopped pineapple
1 cup diced, unpeeled apple   ¼ cup slivered almonds
½ cup finely chopped celery   Mayonnaise

Combine ingredients and serve on bed of salad greens.

BACON AND EGG SALAD

4 cloves garlic, quartered   10 bacon slices
1 cup Oil and Vinegar dressing   1 pound crisp young spinach
3 eggs   greens

Add garlic to the *Oil and Vinegar Dressing*. Hardcook the
eggs and allow them to cool. Fry bacon until crisp and drain
on a brown paper bag. Tear the spinach into small pieces in
a large salad bowl. Chop the eggs and crumble the bacon and
add to the spinach. Pour the dressing over the salad (remove
the garlic cloves) and toss together. Serves six.

RHINELAND RAINBOW

½ pint sour cream   1 cup cabbage, shredded
1 teaspoon horseradish   1 cup apples, diced
2 tablespoons wine vinegar   Lettuce
1 cup pork, cooked and diced   Caraway seeds

Blend sour cream, horseradish, and vinegar. Fold in pork,
cabbage, and apples. Serve on lettuce. Garnish with caraway
seeds.

Thursday/Meats

THREE THURSDAYS SALAD

1 (3-ounce) package plain gelatin
3 tablespoons cold water
2 cups chicken broth
1 (2¼-ounce) can devilled ham

½ cup cottage cheese
¼ cup dill pickle, thinly sliced
Mayonnaise

Soften gelatin in cold water. Bring broth to a boil and dissolve gelatin in broth. Cool. Pour a little of the broth into a mold and chill until it begins to set. Combine ham and cheese and put into mold. Arrange pickle over top, then pour rest of broth over and chill until firm. Garnish with mayonnaise.

LIGHTNING QUICK SALAD

2 cups cut up ham
½ cup diced celery
½ cup finely chopped green onions
½ cup finely chopped bell pepper

Salad greens
Garnish: mayonnaise, mustard,
   olives, sweet gherkins, hardcooked egg

Arrange ham, celery, onions, bell peppers on salad greens on 6 individual plates. Top each with dollop of mayonnaise and an olive. Garnish with gherkin and halved hardcooked egg.

GREENS AU GRATIN

2 tablespoons butter
2 tablespoons flour
½ teaspoon onion, minced
¾ cup milk
1 teaspoon prepared mustard

½ cup Cheddar cheese, grated
Salt and cracked pepper
Mixed salad greens, drained and
   pulled apart
½ cup ham, Julienne-sliced

Melt butter and stir in flour. Cook, stirring, on lowest heat for about 2 minutes. Add onion. Pour in milk and continue to cook, stirring until mixture thickens. Blend in mustard and cheese thoroughly. Season and cool. Lightly toss greens and ham in dressing.

HAWAIIAN HAM SALAD

1 (3-ounce) package lemon
  gelatin
1 cup boiling water
½ cup heavy cream
½ cup mayonnaise
2 tablespoons horseradish

1 (8¼-ounce) can crushed pineapple, drained
½ cup cottage cheese
½ cup pecans
½ cup ham, shredded

Dissolve gelatin in boiling water. Cool slightly. Blend in cream, mayonnaise, and horseradish. Fold in the remaining ingredients and chill until set.

FAR-TO-GO SALAD

1 teaspoon onion, minced
1 teaspoon white wine
2 teaspoons vinegar
1 tablespoon salad oil
½ cup cream

Salt and pepper
1 cup lima beans, cooked
½ cup ham, shredded
1 tablespoon parsley, minced

Blend onion, wine, vinegar, oil and cream. Season. Lightly combine beans and ham with dressing. Garnish with parsley.

Thursday/Meats

Friday's Child
is loving & giving

Friday is Freyja's day, Freyja being the Scandinavian goddess of love. It is thus only fitting that Friday's child be "loving." And since the traditional food for Friday—fish—makes a salad too large for one, it is also fitting for Friday's child to be "giving." These salads are meant to be shared!

Seafoods

Pink Shrimp Salad
Shrimp Boats
California Cocktail
Shrimp Calvados
Shrimp Marinade Medley
Sailboats
Creamy Crab Salad
Thorny Crabs
Crabmeat Aspic
Salmon Loaf Salad
Sunstream Salmon
Clear Salmon Salad
Salmon Mousse
Neptune's Tuna
Sea Shore Salad
Haitian Holiday
Sea Shells

PINK SHRIMP SALAD

1 tablespoon plain gelatin
¼ cup lukewarm water
1 can tomato soup
1 (3-ounce) package cream cheese
1 small cucumber

¼ cup finely chopped onion
¼ cup finely chopped bell pepper
¼ cup finely chopped celery
1 cup cooked shrimp
1 cup heavy cream, whipped

Dissolve gelatin in water over medium heat. Heat the soup and add the cream cheese and then stir in gelatin. Fold in cucumber, onion, bell pepper, celery and shrimp. Fold in whipped cream and pour into a dampened mold. Serves 6.

SHRIMP BOATS

6 eggs, hardcooked
1 cup shrimp, boiled, peeled,
  and coarsely chopped
½ cup mayonnaise

½ teaspoon lemon rind, grated
Salt and white pepper
Mayonnaise
Watercress

Cut eggs in half lengthwise. Scoop out yolks. Blend thoroughly yolks, mayonnaise, lemon and seasoning. Add shrimp to egg yolks. Fill egg halves with mixture. Frost with mayonnaise and garnish with watercress.

CALIFORNIA COCKTAIL

Juice of 1 lemon
½ teaspoon curry powder
4 cups shrimp, cooked, deveined

1 cup slivered almonds
1 cup pineapple chunks, halved
1 cup finely diced celery

Several hours before serving, combine lemon juice and curry powder and pour over shrimp. Toss together. Combine almonds, pineapple, and celery and add to shrimp. Mix lightly. This may be served as a cocktail cup or a salad. No dressing is necessary.

SHRIMP CALVADOS

3 avocados
1 cup shrimp
2 teaspoons onion, minced

Roquefort Dressing
¼ cup pecans, chopped

Split avocados and remove seeds. Combine shrimp and onion with *Roquefort Dressing* and fill the avocado halves. Garnish with pecans.

SHRIMP MARINADE MEDLEY

1½ pounds fresh shrimp, cooked
1 cup finely chopped onion
1 cup fresh parsley, snipped
¾ cup salad oil

¼ cup vinegar
1 clove garlic, minced
1 teaspoon salt
Dash of pepper

Combine the shrimp, onion and parsley in a large bowl. In a small bowl, combine the salad oil, vinegar, garlic, salt and pepper. Mix well and pour over shrimp. Marinate several hours before serving on a bed of salad greens. Serves 6.

SAILBOATS

2 cups lump crabmeat	2 ripe avocados
Lemon Tree Mayonnaise	4 ripe olives
Lemon, halved	2 hardcooked eggs, halved
Lettuce	

Thoroughly pick over the crabmeat. Place in a bowl and squeeze one half lemon over crabmeat. Fold in enough mayonnaise to hold together. Arrange the lettuce on individual plates. Place one half avocado on each and fill each with crabmeat. Garnish with ripe olives and one half hardboiled egg "sail" standing tall.

CREAMY CRAB SALAD

2 tablespoons plain gelatin	1 tablespoon Worcestershire
½ cup cold water	Salt to taste
2 (3-ounce) packages cream cheese	1 (1-pound) carton lump crab-
1 can cream of mushroom soup	meat
1 cup mayonnaise	1 cup celery, finely chopped

Soften gelatin in water. Combine next 5 ingredients in top of a double boiler and heat. Remove from heat and stir in gelatin. Add crabmeat and celery and pour into individual molds which have been rinsed with cold water. Serves 6-8.

THORNY CRABS

1 cup crabmeat	French Dressing made with lemon
1 cup artichoke hearts, chopped	juice
¼ cup celery, finely chopped	Lemon pepper
1 teaspoon onion, minced	Salad greens

Combine crabmeat and vegetables with dressing. Season and chill. Serve on salad greens.

CRABMEAT ASPIC

2 cups tomato juice
Salt and pepper
1 teaspoon vinegar
2 teaspoons onion juice
2 tablespoons plain gelatin
½ cup cold water

1 pound fresh or canned crabmeat
2 stalks celery, finely chopped
1 cup mayonnaise
½ teaspoon onion juice
¼ teaspoon Tabasco
Parsley flakes

In a saucepan, mix the tomato juice, salt, pepper, vinegar, and onion juice together and allow to simmer for 8 to 10 minutes. Soak gelatin in cold water and stir into hot mixture until dissolved. Allow to stand until cooled and fold in crabmeat and celery. Mold and refrigerate. Serve on beds of lettuce and garnish with mayonnaise which has been seasoned with onion juice and Tabasco. Dust with parsley flakes.

SALMON LOAF SALAD

1 tablespoon melted butter
1 teaspoon flour
1 teaspoon salt
1 egg yolk, beaten
½ cup milk
1 tablespoon lemon juice
1 teaspoon grated onion

1 tablespoon plain gelatin
¼ cup cold water
1 can salmon, drained, skin
  removed
Garnish: mayonnaise, chopped
  parsley, grated onion, capers

Combine melted butter, flour, and salt. Heat until mixture bubbles, stirring well. Transfer mixture to double boiler. Stir yolk into milk, blend well and add to butter mixture, using a wire whisk to blend. Cook and stir until mixture begins to thicken. Remove from heat and add lemon juice, onion, and softened gelatin. Blend together and add salmon which has been flaked. Refrigerate in a loaf pan until set, preferably overnight. To serve, place on lettuce bed and garnish with topping made from mayonnaise, parsley and grated onion. Sprinkle with capers. Served with finger sandwiches of cheese, this makes a hearty meal.

SUNSTREAM SALMON

2 (1-pound) cans salmon, drained
2 cups finely chopped celery
½ cup green grapes, halved
½ cup grated onion
¼ cup cut parsley
1 cup mayonnaise
Salt and freshly ground black
  pepper
Spinach leaves

Combine the above ingredients taking care to remove the skin from the salmon. Serve on beds of fresh spinach leaves.

CLEAR SALMON SALAD

1 (3-ounce) package gelatin
3 tablespoons cold water
2 cups beef bouillon
2 bay leaves
1 (15½-ounce) can salmon
½ cup dill pickle, thinly sliced
Lettuce
Mayonnaise

Soften gelatin in cold water. Bring bouillon and bay leaves to a boil. Remove bay leaves. Dissolve gelatin in bouillon. Cool. Arrange salmon and dill pickles in a mold and pour in bouillon. Chill until set. Serve on lettuce and garnish with mayonnaise.

SALMON MOUSSE

1 tablespoon plain gelatin
2 tablespoons cold water
1 tablespoon lemon juice
¾ cup boiling water
1 chicken bouillon cube
1 (15½-ounce) can salmon
1 tablespoon onion, minced
1 tablespoon parsley
1 cup heavy cream, whipped
Salt and pepper

Soften gelatin in cold water and lemon juice. Add bouillon cube to boiling water and stir until dissolved. Then dissolve gelatin in bouillon and blend in salmon, onion, and parsley. Fold in whipped cream and season. Pour into a mold and chill until set.

NEPTUNE'S TUNA

1 (6½-ounce) can tuna
½ cup finely diced celery
1 cup chopped, unpared apples

½ cup broken pecan meats
Juice of ½ lemon
¾ cup mayonnaise

Scald the tuna and allow to drain until all moisture has drained off. Flake with a fork until it is shredded, then combine with remaining ingredients. Serve on a bed of lettuce with crackers, or as sandwich spread.

SEA SHORE SALAD

Lettuce
1 pound fish or shrimp, cooked
3 eggs, hardcooked and sliced
½ cup mayonnaise
2 tablespoons onion, finely
  chopped

2 tablespoons pickle, finely
  chopped
2 teaspoons lemon juice
3 tablespoons heavy cream
Lemon pepper
Parsley

Arrange fish or shrimp on lettuce and surround with sliced eggs. Pour on sauce made by blending the mayonnaise, onion, pickle, lemon juice and cream. Season and chill.

HAITIAN HOLIDAY

3 avocados
1 cup shrimp, cooked, peeled,
  and roughly chopped
¼ cup celery, finely chopped

1 egg, hardcooked, chopped
½ cup mayonnaise
1 tablespoon lime juice
6 black olives, sliced

Cut avocados in half lengthwise. Combine shrimp, celery, and egg with mayonnaise and lime juice. Fill avocado halves with shrimp mixture and garnish with olives.

SEA SHELLS

1½ cups cooked shell macaroni   1 tablespoon white wine
1 cup shrimp, cooked and peeled   1 tablespoon lemon juice
¼ cup celery, chopped   ¼ teaspoon dry mustard
8 stuffed olives, sliced   ¼ teaspoon paprika
½ cup mayonnaise   Lemon pepper

Combine first 4 ingredients. Fold with dressing made by mixing remaining ingredients.

Saturday's Child
works hard for a living

Saturday is for many a day of hard work. Those who have Monday-to-Friday jobs must devote part of Saturday to housework, laundry, marketing, etc. In order to lessen the load and allow for much of the day to be "... jolly old Saturday, mad-as-a-hatter-day, nothing-much-matter-day-night. . ." (Sir Alan Patrick Herbert, *Too Much*), here are salads that are complete meals in themselves.

Meals-in-a-Dish

Ham and Corn Salad
Fleet's In!
Ham and Egg Hayride
Green Rings
Medici
Mad Hatter Salad
Salad Sandwich Loaf
Rainy Day Tuna-Mac
Provencal Salad

Oriental Saturday
Fisherman's Wharf
Day at the Ranch Salad
Beefed-Up Rice
Kaleidoscope
Sunburst
Guadalajara
Hot Potato Salad
A Touch of Austria

HAM AND CORN SALAD

2 cans shoepeg whole kernal corn   1 cup finely chopped bell pepper
1 cup chopped celery   1 small jar pimentoes, cut up
1 cup diced ham   Oil and Vinegar dressing

Combine first 5 ingredients and toss with *Oil and Vinegar* dressing. Allow to chill and place on lettuce leaves on six individual plates.

FLEET'S IN!

2 cans Navy beans   1 cup ham, diced
Small piece salt pork   3 green onions, finely chopped
½ teaspoon sugar   ½ cup cut parsley
Salt and pepper   ¾ cup finely cut bell pepper
1 bay leaf   Oil and Vinegar dressing

Drain and wash beans. Place in saucepan with water to cover. Place pork in skillet and render. Add to beans with grease, salt and pepper, sugar and bay leaf. Cook long enough for beans to absorb meat flavor, but do not allow to overcook. Drain beans, discard fat, allow to cool. Combine with remaining ingredients and blend with *Oil and Vinegar* dressing. Refigerate. Serve on salad greens.

HAM AND EGG HAYRIDE

4 eggs, hardcooked   1 teaspoon wine vinegar
1 cup ham, shredded   1 tablespoon oil
2 cups cooked rice   2 tablespoons chutney
½ cup mayonnaise   Salt and lemon pepper
2 tablespoons catsup   Parsley

Combine ham and rice. Split eggs lengthwise and arrange halves on rice. Cover with dressing made by combining next 6 ingredients. Garnish with parsley.

GREEN RINGS

2 cups cooked ham, diced
1 cup celery, finely chopped
1 cup cooked macaroni
2 hardcooked eggs, chopped
½ cup sweet pickle relish
1 cup mayonnaise

1 tablespoon creole mustard
¼ cup sour cream
6 medium-sized bell peppers,
  washed and cored
Horseradish Sauce
Lettuce and tomato wedges

Combine first 8 ingredients and fold together until well blended. Stuff the peppers and refrigerate until chilled. Slice the peppers crosswise and place on beds of lettuce leaves. Top with *Horseradish Sauce* and garnish with tomato wedges.

MEDICI

2 cups spinach noodles, cooked
  and drained
1 cup ham, Julienne-sliced
1 cup Swiss cheese, Julienne-
  sliced
¾ cup mayonnaise

¼ cup chili sauce
2 tablespoons salad oil
1 tablespoon lemon juice
2 teaspoons mustard
Salt and pepper
Black olives

Lightly combine noodles, ham, cheese, and carrots with dressing made of next 6 ingredients. Garnish with olives.

MAD HATTER SALAD

3 cups cooked rice, cooled
¾ cup chopped green onions
¾ cup sliced radishes
1 cup diced ham
1 (7-ounce) can corn, drained

½ cup chopped bell pepper
2 tablespoons chopped parsley
½ cup finely chopped celery
Salt and pepper
Salad dressing of choice

Combine all ingredients and fold together with your choice of dressings.

SALAD SANDWICH LOAF

2½ cups chicken or tuna salad
1 small loaf day-old bread,
  unsliced
Mayonnaise
Lettuce, torn into bite-size pieces

1 (8-ounce) package cream cheese,
  softened
3 tablespoons cream
Stuffed olives
Parsley

Remove crust from the bread loaf. Slice the loaf into four slices lengthwise. Spread with mayonnaise. On three slices, arrange the cut-up lettuce and cover with the salad to make 3 layers. Put the top on and press the whole loaf firmly. A weight may be placed on top. Mash the cream cheese and mix in enough cream to make it spreadable. Cover the loaf on the top and sides. A garnish of sliced stuffed olives may be used. Chill. To serve, place on platter, surround with parsley. Cut in thick slices. Serves 6 - 8.

RAINY DAY TUNA-MAC

1 (6½-ounce) can tuna, drained
2 cups cooked macaroni
2 slices Swiss cheese, shredded

½ cup pimento, chopped
¾ cup mayonnaise
Salt and pepper

Combine the ingredients, season, and chill 2 to 3 hours before serving.

PROVENCAL SALAD

Bibb lettuce
1 cup potatoes, cooked, diced
1 cup green beans
1 large tomato, skinned
1 (6½-ounce) can tuna, drained

2 hardcooked eggs, cut into
  wedges
Black olives
Anchovies
French Dressing

On a large plate, arrange vegetables, tuna, and eggs in alternate sections on a bed of lettuce. Garnish with olives and anchovies. Pour on dressing.

ORIENTAL SATURDAY

2 cups shrimp, boiled, deveined
  and cut up
1 cup celery, finely chopped
½ cup grated onion
½ cup finely chopped bell pepper
¾ cup seedless raisins

3 cups rice, cooked and cooled
3 tablespoons lemon juice
½ cup salad oil
Lettuce leaves
Sliced cucumbers, unpeeled

Combine first 6 ingredients. Toss with lemon juice and oil.
Arrange lettuce leaves in a bed, add the salad mixture and
garnish with cucumber.

FISHERMAN'S WHARF

1 cup broccoli flowerets, cooked
  slightly, still crisp
1 cup cauliflower flowerets,
  cooked slightly, still crisp
1 (10-ounce) package frozen
  English peas, thawed, uncooked
2 cups shrimp, cooked, peeled,
  and deveined

½ cup capers
½ cup shaved mild cheese
1 cup Butter Churn Croutons
1 head iceberg lettuce, shredded
6 spinach leaves, torn
Salt and pepper
Italian or French Dressing

Combine all ingredients in large salad bowl and toss lightly
with *Italian* or *French* dressing. *French II* with tomato base
is excellent.

Saturday/Meals-in-a-Dish
53

DAY AT THE RANCH SALAD

Lettuce and spinach leaves, torn
2 cups thinly-sliced slivers of
  roast beef
3 tomatoes, quartered

1 cup shaved sharp cheese
1½ cups Butter Churn Croutons
Oil and Vinegar *dressing*
3 finely chopped hardcooked eggs

Toss all ingredients except egg with *Oil and Vinegar* dressing. Arrange on individual salad plates; top with egg. Serves 6.

BEEFED-UP RICE

1 cup cooked roast beef,
  Julienne-sliced
2 cups cooked rice
3 tablespoons chopped bell pepper
3 tablespoons chopped celery
¼ cup dill pickle, chopped

DRESSING:
4 teaspoons red wine vinegar
3 tablespoons oil
1 teaspoon mustard
½ teaspoon horseradish
Salt and pepper

Lightly combine the salad ingredients with the dressing.

KALEIDOSCOPE

Vinaigrette *dressing*
¼ teaspoon mixed herbs
2 cups new potatoes, boiled
  and diced
1 cup sour cream
1 tablespoon lemon juice

1 cup cooked veal, Julienne-
  sliced
1 (8-ounce) can mushrooms
1 (8½-ounce) can English peas
½ cup pecans, chopped
Salt and pepper

Add herbs to *Viniagrette* dressing and cover potatoes. Let stand for at least half an hour. Combine sour cream and lemon juice. Drain potatoes. Lightly toss potatoes, veal, mushrooms, peas, pecans, salt and pepper with cream dressing.

SUNBURST

1 package frozen small lima beans
1 package frozen English peas
1 can French-style green beans
½ small onion, grated
1¼ cups Lemon Tree Mayonnaise
¼ cup olive oil
¼ teaspoon creole mustard
1 tablespoon lemon juice
½ teaspoon Worcestershire

Few drops Tabasco
4 hardcooked eggs, separated and
  finely chopped
1 cup grated sharp cheese
Lettuce and spinach greens
Green tops of 3 green onions,
  finely chopped
Fresh snipped parsley

Prepare the vegetables, cooking the frozen ones until barely done and rinsing and washing the canned beans. Place them in a large bowl. Combine the next 8 ingredients and lightly toss with the vegetables. Refrigerate until thoroughly chilled, overnight, if possible. When ready to serve, prepare a shallow bowl with a bed of lettuce and spinach greens. Spoon on the vegetable mixture. Arrange the green onions in a small circle in the center, the egg whites around the onions, and the yellows around the whites. Follow with the shaved cheese around the yolks and garnish with fresh parsley. Beautiful!

GUADALAJARA

1 pound ground round, cooked,
  seasoned and drained
1 head of lettuce, torn into
  small pieces
8 leaves of spinach, torn
2 - 3 small pieces of chicory, torn
1 can red kidney beans, washed
  and drained

2 tomatoes, cut into quarters
2 avocados, cut up
1 cup American cheese, grated
½ cup Oil and Vinegar dressing
1 cup Thousand Island dressing
½ cup broken pieces of tortilla
  chips
½ cup sliced ripe olives

Combine the first 8 ingredients. Toss with *Oil and Vinegar* dressing. Add *Thousand Island* dressing and toss again. Garnish with the chips and olives. A Mexican fiesta in a bowl!

HOT POTATO SALAD

8 large potatoes, sliced, boiled,
and cooled
Salt and pepper
½ cup finely chopped celery
½ cup finely chopped green
onions (optional)
½ cup finely chopped bell pepper

2 tablespoons finely chopped
parsley
3 tablespoons lemon juice
1 tablespoon vinegar
5 tablespoons olive oil
½ cup crisp bacon, crumbled

Salt and pepper the potatoes to taste. Add remaining ingredients except bacon and toss lightly. Place in a casserole and put in 350-degree oven just long enough to heat. Garnish with bacon. Serves 6.

A TOUCH OF AUSTRIA

6 large baking potatoes, boiled,
cooled and cut up
Juice of one lemon
Salt and pepper
6 green onions, finely chopped
1 bell pepper, finely chopped
1 stalk celery, finely chopped

3 hardcooked eggs, cut into
small pieces
1½ cups mayonnaise
1 tablespoon mustard
1 teaspoon Durkee's salad
dressing
1 small can Vienna sausages

Spread the pototoes on a platter. Squeeze the lemon over them and sprinkle with salt and pepper. Place in large bowl along with onions, pepper, celery, eggs and Vienna sausages. In another bowl, fold together mayonnaise, mustard and Durkee's dressing. Add to potato mixture and toss lightly until well blended. Be careful not to mash potatoes. Sweet or dill pickle may be added if desired. The secret to good potato salad is to allow it to absorb the flavors for several hours before serving.

Sunday's Child

is bonnie & blythe, and good & gay

Fortunate is Sunday's child born on that day "betwixt a Saturday and a Monday," for it is bonnie and blythe and good and gay. Of all the salads, the favorite of children is one of fruit, especially ones like *Strawberry Fair* or *Child's Play*—so good they can also be dessert!

Fruits

Caribbean Fruit
Florida Garden
Golden Hoard
Child's Play
Summer Delight
The Orange and the Green
Cool As A Cucumber
Sparkling Fruit
Westwind Lime
Sunshine
Cherry Red Wine

Health Nut
Blueberry Cream Delight
Dessert, Too
Pineapple-Apple Salad
Cranberry Sunday
Sun Spin
Sunday Best Frozen Fruit Salad
Looks Like Snow
Wink-of-an-Eye Salad
Winter Fruit
Coke and a Smile Salad

Georgia Farm Salad
Waldorf Salad
Strawberry Fair

CARIBBEAN FRUIT

2 cups rice, cooked
2 bananas, sliced
½ cup celery, chopped
½ cup bell pepper, chopped
½ cup almonds, toasted
¼ cup raisins

¼ cup mayonnaise
¼ cup whipping cream, whipped
1 tablespoon salad oil
2 tablespoons lemon juice
2 tablespoons honey

Lightly combine rice, bananas, celery, bell pepper, almonds and raisins with dressing made by blending mayonnaise, cream, oil, juice and honey. Tropically delightful!

FLORIDA GARDEN

½ head iceberg lettuce
10 leaves of spinach
2 cucumbers

1 grapefruit, peeled and sectioned
Avocado Dressing

Wash lettuce and spinach thoroughly, drain and chill in crisper. Tear lettuce and spinach and place in a salad bowl. Seed the cucumbers, shave with a potato peeler and add to the lettuce and spinach. Add the grapefruit sections and toss. Arrange on individual salad plates and cover with *Avocado Dressing*. Serves six.

GOLDEN HOARD

1 bunch endive
2 oranges, thinly sliced
½ cup cashew nuts
1 onion, thinly sliced

½ cup salad oil
2 tablespoons vinegar
1 tablespoon lemon juice
Dashes of sugar, garlic salt

Toss first 4 ingredients in a dressing made of remaining ingredients.

CHILD'S PLAY

2 apples, diced
1 (11-ounce) can Mandarin orange
  segments, drained
1 cup miniature marshmallows
½ cup pecans

1¼ cup celery, chopped
¼ cup mayonnaise
½ cup whipped topping
1 tablespoon orange juice

Combine the first five ingredients with the dressing made by blending the mayonnaise, whipped topping and orange juice. The amount of dressing needed may vary depending on the size of the apples.

SUMMER DELIGHT

Salad greens
1 cup diced apples
3 bananas, quartered
1 cup melon balls
1 cup strawberries, halved
1 cup seedless grapes

Juice of 1 lemon
2 oranges, sectioned
2 cups sour cream
2 tablespoons honey
¼ cup poppy seeds
6 whole strawberries

Arrange salad greens on six dinner plates. Combine the next 5 ingredients, sprinkle with the juice of a lemon and toss. Arrange on the beds of greens. Fold together the orange sections, sour cream, honey and poppy seeds. Pour over the fruit and garnish with the strawberries.

THE ORANGE AND THE GREEN

Shredded lettuce
1 avocado, sliced
2 oranges, peeled and thinly sliced

½ small onion, thinly sliced
¼ cup cashew nuts
French Dressing

Lightly toss the first five ingredients with the dressing.

COOL AS A CUCUMBER

1 (3-ounce) package lemon
  gelatin
1 cup cottage cheese

1 cup seedless grapes
½ cup cucumber, diced
1 tablespoon mint, finely chopped

Prepare gelatin according to instructions. When it has begun to thicken, lightly stir in remaining ingredients. Really takes the heat off a summer day!

SPARKLING FRUIT

1 can black cherries
1 large can crushed pineapple,
  drained
1 large package raspberry gelatin

2 small bottles club soda
1 (8-ounce) package cream cheese
1 cup pecans, chopped

Drain both cans of fruit, reserving the juice. Boil juice and pour over gelatin, stirring until dissolved. Add club soda. Soften cream cheese and beat until fluffy. Combine with the pecans and stir into the gelatin. Combine with the fruit and pour into molds.

WESTWIND LIME

1 (3-ounce) package lime gelatin
1 cup boiling water
½ cup cottage cheese
¼ cup finely chopped pecans

1 small can crushed pineapple
  and juice
1 tablespoon horseradish
½ cup grated strong cheese

Dissolve the gelatin in boiling water and combine with the remaining ingredients. Pour into molds and refriderate until set. Serve on lettuce; dress with mayonnaise.

SUNSHINE

1 (3-ounce) package lemon gelatin
½ cup carrots, grated
¼ cup bell pepper, finely chopped
½ cup cabbage, shredded
1 cup pineapple, crushed and
  drained, reserving juice

Prepare gelatin according to directions using pineapple juice for part of the liquid. Fold in the vegetables and pineapple. Pour into a mold and chill until set. Serve garnished with mayonnaise.

CHERRY RED WINE

1 (3-ounce) package cherry
  gelatin
1½ cups boiling water
½ cup Port or Hearty Burgundy
½ cup celery, chopped
1 cup pecans, chopped
8 ounces cream cheese, softened
  with 1 tablespoon mayonnaise
1 (16-ounce) can dark cherries

Dissolve gelatin in boiling water. Add the wine and cool. When the gelatin begins to set, blend the celery, pecans and cream cheese into half the gelatin. Pour into a mold and chill until firm. Add the cherries to the other half of the gelatin to form the second layer. Chill until set.

HEALTH NUT

8 carrots, grated
2 tart apples, pared and diced
½ cup seedless raisins
½ to ¾ cup mayonnaise
½ cup slivered almonds

Fold all ingredients together. Serves six.

BLUEBERRY CREAM DELIGHT

1 (3-ounce) package black raspberry gelatin
½ cup boiling water
¼ cup ice-cold water
1 tablespoon lemon juice

¼ teaspoon lemon zest
1 (21-ounce) can blueberry pie
  filling
1 cup sour cream
¼ cup powdered sugar

Dissolve gelatin in boiling water. Add cold water, lemon juice and lemon zest. Cool. Stir into pie filling. Pour into a mold and chill until set. Blend sugar into sour cream and spread on gelatin. Chill thoroughly. Serve on lettuce for salad—or mold in a graham cracker pie shell for dessert!

DESSERT, TOO

1 banana, sliced
1 cup coconut
1 cup mandarin oranges, drained
1 cup miniature marshmallows

1 cup pineapple, crushed
½ cup pecans, chopped
1 cup sour cream

Lightly combine all the ingredients and chill. A superb salad to accompany any meal—and it's a delicious "dessert, too."

PINEAPPLE-APPLE SALAD

6 yellow Delicious apples
½ cup celery, finely chopped
½ cup crushed pineapple,
  drained

½ cup pecans, chopped
½ pint whipping cream, whipped,
  and lightly sweetened
1 tablespoon lemon juice

Slice off the tops of apples and core them. Carefully scoop out some of the apple to be diced, but leave enough to form a shell. Combine diced apple, celery, crushed pineapple, and pecans with lemon juice. Fold fruit into whipped cream and fill apple cases.

CRANBERRY SUNDAY

1 package fresh cranberries,
  ground or processed
1 large can crushed pineapple,
  drained, juice reserved
1 large package raspberry gelatin
½ cup sugar
2 cups boiling water

½ cup cold club soda
Juice of one lemon
1 orange, sectioned, then put
  through blender or processor
1 cup sliced water chestnuts
1 cup pecans, finely chopped

Prepare cranberries and pineapple. Combine gelatin and sugar. Add boiling water and stir until dissolved. Add club soda, lemon juice and pineapple juice. Place in refrigerator until it has partially jelled. Fold in the pineapple, cranberries, orange, water chestnuts and pecans. Pour into mold and chill until firm. Makes any Sunday a holiday!

SUN SPIN

1 (16-ounce) can grapefruit sections
1 (12-ounce) can unsweetened
  grapefruit juice

2 tablespoons plain gelatin
2 tablespoons lemon juice
1 large avocado, peeled and sliced

Drain grapefruit sections reserving juice. Soften gelatin in ½ cup grapefruit juice and dissolve in ½ cup boiling grapefruit juice and lemon juice. Add to rest of juice and juice from can of sections. When gelatin begins to thicken, arrange grapefruit sections and avocado slices in "sun spins" in mold. Pour gelatin over fruit and chill until set. Serve garnished with mayonnaise.

Sunday/Fruits

63

SUNDAY BEST FROZEN FRUIT SALAD

1 (20-ounce) can sliced pineapple
1 (10-ounce) bottle maraschino
   cherries
1 (17-ounce) can fruit cocktail
Juice of 2 lemons
12 marshmallows
1 tablespoon plain gelatin

5 drops red food coloring
4 tablespoons sugar
4 tablespoons flour
Dash of salt
4 large bananas
¼ cup mayonnaise
1¼ cups whipping cream, whipped

Drain fruit and reserve the juice. Combine the pineapple, cherry and lemon juices, adding enough juice from fruit cocktail to make 2 cups of juice. Heat juice and stir in marshmallows until melted. Add coloring. Soften gelatin in 4 tablespoons of juice from fruit cocktail and dissolve in hot juice. Mix sugar and flour and add enough hot juice to make a thin paste. Slowly stir paste into hot juice. Cook until mixture thickens and becomes transparent. Add salt. Let mixture cool completely.

Cut pineapple and cherries into small pieces and add to fruit cocktail. Add fruit to cooled juice. Mash bananas into a paste and mix in mayonnaise; blend in fruit mixture and fold in whipped cream. Freeze in freezer containers. When ready to serve, slice as many portions as needed and return the rest to freezer.

LOOKS LIKE SNOW

1 can fruit cocktail
Handful maraschino cherries
1 small can crushed pineapple
1 (3-ounce) package cream cheese

2 cups miniature marshmallows
½ pint whipping cream, whipped
¾ cup mayonnaise

Fold all ingredients together gently, place in mold and freeze. Simply scrumptious!

WINK-OF-AN-EYE SALAD

1 (15¼-ounce) can pineapple slices
  or chunks, or pear halves
Lettuce

Grated cheese
Mayonnaise
4 maraschino cherries

Chill canned fruit in freezer at least 10 minutes. Then place fruit atop lettuce on 4 individual salad plates. Sprinkle generously with grated cheese. Top with scoop of mayonnaise and a cherry. Quick elegance when company drops in.

WINTER FRUIT

1 orange, thinly sliced
1 apple, diced
¼ cup celery, chopped
½ cup dates, chopped
¼ cup walnuts or pecans

½ cup plain yogurt OR
½ cup mayonnaise plus 1 teaspoon lemon juice OR
2 tablespoons mayonnaise
  plus ½ cup whipped topping

Mix all together with desired amount of mayonnaise and lemon juice or whipped topping or yogurt.

COKE AND A SMILE SALAD

1 tablespoon plain gelatin
Juice of ½ lemon, plus enough
  to make ¼ cup
1¾ cups Coca Cola

¼ cup pecans, chopped
1 (3-ounce) package cream cheese,
  cut into small pieces
1 cup seedless grapes, halved

Soften gelatin in lemon juice and water. Heat ½ cup Coca Cola to the boil and add gelatin. Stir until dissolved. Add gelatin to rest of the Coca Cola. Pour into a mold and chill until thickened. Fold in pecans, cream cheese and grapes and chill until set. Garnish with dollop of mayonnaise.

GEORGIA FARM SALAD

2 apples, diced
1 tablespoon lemon juice
½ cup peanuts

½ cup cabbage, shredded
Mayonnaise

Combine the apples with the lemon juice. Lightly mix the apples, peanuts and cabbage with the mayonnaise.

WALDORF SALAD

2 cups diced, unpared apples
1 cup finely chopped celery

¾ cup broken pecan meats
¾ cup mayonnaise

Combine the above ingredients and gently fold together. Serve on a bed of lettuce.

STRAWBERRY FAIR

Shredded lettuce
1 cup strawberries, halved

1 cucumber, thinly sliced
Poppy Seed Dressing

Arrange strawberry halves on slices of cucumber on a bed of shredded lettuce. Pour on dressing.

Sunday/Fruits

Everyday

All the salads of the week will burst into life with the dressings and sauces listed in this section. Most cream dressings, tightly contained and refrigerated, will keep for weeks; oil and vinegar dressings, for months. Home-made dressings are not only economical and easy to prepare, but are made of your own choice of fresh ingredients.

Dressings

Vinaigrette
Italian Dressing
Creamy Italian
Anglo-Norman Dressing
Green Goddess
French Dressing
French II
Oil and Vinegar
Thousand Island
Avocado Dressing
Avocado II

Roquefort or Blue Cheese Dressing
Strawberry Sunrise Dressing
Poppy Seed Dressing
Celery Seed Dressing
Yogurt Dressing
Apricot Curry Cream
Tarragon Cream
Remoulade Sauce
Horseradish Sauce
Lemon Tree Mayonnaise
Secret Spring Dressing

Cooked Salad Cream
Buttermilk Sky Dressing
Sour Cream Plus
Louis Dressing
Butter Churn Croutons

VINAIGRETTE

1 cup salad oil
5 tablespoons vinegar OR
  3 tablespoons vinegar plus
  2 tablespoons lemon juice

1 clove garlic
1½ teaspoons mustard
1½ teaspoons salt
½ teaspoon pepper

Crush garlic with salt. Add mustard and pepper. Beat in oil by tablespoons alternately with vinegar. Refrigerate overnight. Remove garlic, if milder flavor is desired.

ITALIAN DRESSING

1¼ cups olive oil
¼ cup lemon juice
¼ cup tarragon vinegar
2 garlic cloves, crushed
1 teaspoon salt
1 teaspoon ground pepper

1 teaspoon sugar
¼ cup parsley flakes
1 teaspoon crushed basil leaves
¼ cup Parmesan cheese, grated
1 very small onion, halved

Blend all ingredients in blender or processor. Refrigerate.

CREAMY ITALIAN

¼ cup lemon juice
¾ cup salad oil
¾ cup light cream
1 clove garlic, pressed

¼ teaspoon sugar
¼ teaspoon white pepper
Salt to taste

Process or blend thoroughly. Refrigerate.

ANGLO-NORMAN DRESSING

3 tablespoons salad oil
1 tablespoon wine vinegar
¼ teaspoon salt

Dash dry mustard
Dash pepper

Blend all ingredients thoroughly. Quick one-salad dressing.

GREEN GODDESS

2 tablespoons lemon juice
1 cup mayonnaise
½ cup light cream
4 tablespoons wine vinegar
1 clove garlic, pressed

1 tablespoon anchovy paste
1 tablespoon parsley flakes
½ small onion, grated
Freshly ground black pepper
Few drops Tabasco

Combine the lemon juice, mayonnaise and cream until well blended. Add remaining ingredients. Refrigerate till needed.

FRENCH DRESSING

1 cup salad oil
5 tablespoons wine vinegar
1 tablespoon sugar
½ teaspoon salt

½ teaspoon dry mustard
½ teaspoon paprika
1 clove garlic, pressed (optional)

Blend first 6 ingredients thoroughly. Add garlic if desired. Store in a tightly covered jar in refrigerator.

FRENCH II

½ cup condensed cream of
   tomato soup
6 tablespoons white vinegar
¾ cup olive oil
½ clove garlic

1 very small onion, halved
½ cup sugar
1 tablespoon dry mustard
1 tablespoon Worcestershire
Salt and fresh black pepper

Blend and process all ingredients until creamy.

OIL AND VINEGAR

2 tablespoons white vinegar OR
   1 tablespoon vinegar and 1
   tablespoon lemon juice

¾ cup salad oil
Salt and freshly ground pepper

Combine all ingredients in jar and shake well.

THOUSAND ISLAND

2 cups mayonnaise
¼ cup chili sauce
¼ cup catsup
½ cup sweet relish
Juice of one lemon

2 tablespoons soy sauce
1 tablespoon Worcestershire
1 garlic clove, pressed
4 tablespoons grated onion

Put all ingredients into a blender and blend until smooth. Will keep indefinitely in refrigerator.

AVOCADO DRESSING

2 ripe avocados, pureed
Juice of one lemon
¼ cup sour cream
¾ cup mayonnaise
½ cup olive oil

1 teaspoon sugar
½ teaspoon salt
¼ teaspoon Tabasco
1 clove garlic, pressed
½ teaspoon grated onion and juice

Combine all ingredients and mix well. Store tightly covered in refrigerator.

AVOCADO II

½ cup orange juice
½ lemon, skin and seeds removed
2 tablespoons mayonnaise

1 ripe avocado, cut up
Salt to taste

Put all ingredients in blender and process until creamy.

ROQUEFORT OR BLUE CHEESE DRESSING

1 quart mayonnaise
Juice of 3 lemons
1 small onion, grated
½ cup sour cream
½ cup parsley flakes

2 cloves garlic, pressed
1 pound Roquefort or blue
  cheese, crumbled
Salt and freshly ground black
  pepper

Mix all together in large bowl with wire whisk. Refrigerate.

STRAWBERRY SUNRISE DRESSING
(for fresh fruit salad)

1 cup fresh strawberries, sliced
½ cup sugar
½ cup red raspberry jelly
5 tablespoons water

4 teaspoons cornstarch
2 tablespoons cold water
2 tablespoons lemon juice

Bring strawberries, sugar, jelly, and 5 tablespoons water to a boil. Simmer for 15 minutes. Blend cornstarch into 2 tablespoons water, and add to the fruit. Cook until clear and thick. Stir in lemon juice. Chill. Delicious on ice cream!

POPPY SEED DRESSING

¾ cup honey
1 teaspoon dry mustard
1 tablespoon onion, minced
1 cup oil

¼ cup white vinegar
1 tablespoon lemon or lime juice
2 teaspoons poppy seeds
¼ teaspoon salt

Blend ingredients thoroughly.

CELERY SEED DRESSING
(for fresh fruit)

½ cup sugar
1 teaspoon dry mustard
1 teaspoon salt
¼ teaspoon cracked pepper

½ small onion, grated
¼ cup vinegar
¾ cup salad oil
1 tablespoon celery seed

Add a small amount of vinegar to the dry ingredients. Add oil, slowly beating after each addition. Add remaining vinegar and celery seed. Pretty to add red food coloring.

YOGURT DRESSING

1 cup fruit-flavored yogurt
¼ cup mayonnaise

1 tablespoon lemon juice

Blend the ingredients and use for fruit salads. Refrigerate.

APRICOT CURRY CREAM
(for fruit, chicken, or ham salad)

1 teaspoon curry powder
1 small jar babyfood apricots

2 tablespoons white wine
½ pint whipping cream, whipped

Combine curry powder, apricots and wine in a double boiler. Cook, stirring, until thoroughly blended. Allow to cool. Fold in whipped cream. Refrigerate.

TARRAGON CREAM

1 egg, beaten
3 tablespoons sugar
4 tablespoons tarragon vinegar

½ cup whipping cream, whipped
Salt and white pepper

Combine egg and sugar in top of double boiler. Gradually stir in vinegar and continue stirring until mixture thickens. Cool. Fold in whipped cream and season.

REMOULADE SAUCE

1 cup finely chopped green onions
1 cup finely chopped celery
½ cup finely chopped Kosher
  dill pickles
1 garlic clove, pressed

2 cups mustard
1 teaspoon paprika
¼ cup vinegar
Juice of one lemon
1 cup salad oil

Mix all ingredients together and store in refrigerator.

HORSERADISH SAUCE

2 cups sour cream
½ cup horseradish

Juice of half lemon
Salt and pepper

Blend thoroughly. Refrigerate.

LEMON TREE MAYONNAISE

1 egg
½ teaspoon vinegar
1 teaspoon Dijon mustard
1 teaspoon lemon juice

1¼ cups salad oil
½ teaspoon salt
½ teaspoon lemon juice

Combine egg, vinegar, mustard, 1 teaspoon lemon juice and 1 tablespoon salad oil in food processor or small, deep bowl. With processor or rotary beater or slowest speed of hand mixer, mix for 1 minute. Without stopping mixer, add oil very slowly, literally drop by drop, until it has thickened. Add salt and ½ teaspoon lemon juice. Perfectly scrumptious!

SECRET SPRING DRESSING

1 (2-ounce) can anchovies
4 stalks celery
¼ medium onion
3 cloves garlic
1 tablespoon whole peppercorns

1 teaspoon Accent
2½ cups salad oil
1 teaspoon mustard
3 eggs

Process in food processor or cut finely anchovies, celery, onion, garlic, and grind peppercorns. Mix in processor or blender everything but eggs for one minute. Add whole eggs one at a time. Blend again thoroughly. Differently delicious!

COOKED SALAD CREAM

¾ teaspoon dry mustard
3 tablespoons sugar
½ teaspoon salt
1½ tablespoons corn starch

½ cup cold water
1 egg
¼ cup vinegar
2 tablespoons butter

Combine dry ingredients and slowly add water. In top of a double boiler, beat together the egg and vinegar. Add the dissolved ingredients and cook, stirring, until thick and smooth. Add butter and chill.

BUTTERMILK SKY DRESSING

1 cup mayonnaise
1 cup sour cream
½ cup buttermilk
½ small onion, grated
¼ teaspoon garlic salt OR
  1 clove garlic, pressed

2 tablespoons chopped parsley
Juice of ½ lemon
1 tablespoon soy sauce
4 drops Tabasco
Salt and freshly ground black
  pepper

Shake in quart jar. Store tightly. Refrigerate.

SOUR CREAM PLUS

1 cup sour cream
½ cup cucumber, finely chopped
2 green onions, finely chopped

2 tablespoons bell pepper, finely
  chopped
Lemon pepper

Blend all ingredients thoroughly. Refrigerate.

LOUIS DRESSING

1 cup mayonnaise
¼ cup chili sauce
1 tablespoon tarragon vinegar
½ teaspoon Worcestershire

½ teaspoon Worcestershire
1 small onion, halved
2 tablespoons parsley flakes
6 stuffed olives, finely chopped

Place all ingredients in blender except olives. Blend. Add olives. Chill until used.

BUTTER CHURN CROUTONS

6 slices stale bread, cubed
4 tablespoons butter

Dashes of seasoned salt, garlic
  salt, red pepper, lemon pepper

Melt butter in large skillet. Add seasonings, then add bread cubes all at once and stir to coat evenly. Spread on cookie sheet and bake 10 minutes in 325-degree oven, then turn it off and leave them in the oven for several hours. Children love these—a good way to introduce them to salads is to include these.

INDEX

Coke and a Smile Salad 65
Cool As A Cucumber 60
Cranberry Sunday 63
Dessert, Too 62
Florida Garden 58
Georgia Farm Salad 66
Golden Hoard 58
Health Nut 61
Looks Like Snow 64
The Orange and the Green 59
Pineapple-Apple Salad 62
Sparkling Fruit 60
Strawberry Fair 66
Summer Delight 59
Sunday Best Frozen Fruit
  Salad 64
Sun Spin 61
Sunshine 61
Waldorf Salad 66
Westwind Lime 60
Wink-of-an-Eye Salad 65
Winter Fruit 65

DRESSINGS

Anglo-Norman Dressing 68

Apricot Curry Cream 72
Avocado Dressing 70
Avocado II 70
Butter Churn Croutons 74
Buttermilk Sky Dressing 74
Celery Seed Dressing 71
Cooked Salad Cream 73
Creamy Italian 68
French Dressing 69
French II 69
Green Goddess 69
Horseradish Sauce 72
Italian Dressing 68
Lemon Tree Mayonnaise 73
Louis Dressing 74
Oil and Vinegar 69
Poppy Seed Dressing 71
Remoulade Sauce 72
Roquefort or Blue Cheese
  Dressing 70
Secret Spring Dressing 73
Sour Cream Plus 74
Strawberry Sunrise Dressing 71
Tarragon Cream 72
Thousand Island 70
Vinaigrette 68
Yogurt Dressing 71

Other books by Ruth Moorman and Lalla Williams:

Chocolate lovers readily admit that anything as good as chocolate must be sinful! True chocoholics *lust* for chocolate candy, *envy* their neighbor's cocoa cake, get *greedy* for one more chocolaty cookie. Some are as *proud* as "Chocolate Milk Punch," while others will become *slothful* if they eat too much "Sell-Your-Soul Pudding." There are redeeming recipes such as "Angel Pie" and "Bishop's Bread," and illustrations of debonaire devils and heavenly angels throughout!
$4.95

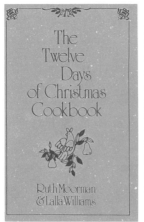

Each of the Twelve Days of Christmas has its appropriate menu celebration. The fifth day features a bridge luncheon with "Golden Ring Slaw" and "Chicken a la Reine on Cranberry Ring" when *my true love gave to me, five golden rings* . . . and piping hot tea for the *eleven pipers piping* along with "Scotch Lace Wafers" and "Dundee Cake." Colorful red and green Christmas illustrations lend a warm holiday spirit to suggested menus for coffees, buffets, midnight breakfasts, etc. $4.95

The Quail Ridge Press Cookbook Series:

THE SEVEN CHOCOLATE SINS $4.95
THE TWELVE DAYS OF CHRISTMAS COOKBOOK $4.95
ANY TIME'S A PARTY! $4.95
QUICKIES FOR SINGLES $4.95
HORS D'OEUVRES EVERYBODY LOVES $4.95
THE COUNTRY MOUSE $4.95
A SALAD A DAY $4.95
BEST OF THE BEST FROM MISSISSIPPI $9.95
BEST OF THE BEST FROM LOUISIANA $9.95

If these books are not available from a local merchant, they
may be ordered directly from:

DISTRIBUTED BY:
Homestead Publishing, Inc.
10500 N. Port Washington Road
Mequon, WI 53092
                1-800-922-6401